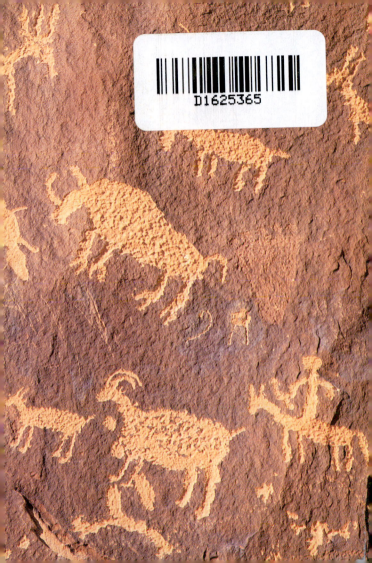

Other Helen Exley giftbooks:

Thoughts on... BEING HAPPY   **Words of Comfort**
Thoughts on... BEING AT PEACE   **The Best of Nature Quotations**

Published simultaneously in 1997 by Exley Publications in Great Britain,
and Exley Giftbooks in the USA.

12 11 10 9 8 7 6 5 4 3

ISBN 1-8505-838-X

**Exley Publications Ltd., 16 Chalk Hill, Watford,
Herts WD1 4BN, United Kingdom.
Exley Publications LLC, 232 Madison Avenue, Suite 1409,
NY 10016, USA.**

A copy of the CIP data is available from the British Library on request.

Edited by Helen Exley.
Pictures researched by Image Select International.
Typeset by Delta, Watford.
Printed in China.

Picture Credits: The Bridgeman Art Library (BAL), Images Colour Library (ICL),
Gamma (GA), Tony Stone Images (TSI), Superstock (SS). Cover, p 58: George Catlin, He
Who Has Eyes Behind Him, BAL; Endpapers: Petroglyphs, ICL; Title Page, p 35: George
Catlin, The Twin, Wife of Bloody Hand, BAL; p 11: An Indian Gathering, GA; p 15:
Albert Bierstadt,The Sierra Nevada Mountains, BAL; p 19: Phil Borges, Blackfoot
Woman, TSI; p 22/23: The Grand Canyon, ICL; p 26/27: GA; p 30/31: Steve Bly, Native
Americans, TSI; p 39: J.H. Sharp, The Medicine Man, SS; p 41: Petroglyph, ICL; p 45:
Thomas Moran, Cliffs of Upper Colorado, BAL; p 48-49: Thomas Moran, The Miracles of
Nature, BAL; p 52: Greg Gorman, Floyd Red Crow, GA; p 54: The Valley of the Gods,
ICL, p 56: Phil Borges, Portrait of American Indian, TSI; p 61: Petroglyphs, ICL.
Acknowledgements: The publishers are grateful for permission to reproduce copyright
material. Whilst every effort has been made to trace copyright holders translators, the
publishers would be pleased to hear from any not here acknowledged. BLACK ELK:
Extracts from *Black Elk: Being the Life Story of a Holy Man of the Oglala Sioux* by John G.
Neihardt. Published by the University of Nebraska Press. WALKING BUFFALO: Extracts
from *Tanga Mani, Walking Buffalo of the Stories*, by Grant Mac Ewan, M. J. Hurtig Ltd,
Edmonton. 1969. BLACKFEET BANDS CHIEF: Extract from *Bury My Heart at Wounded
Knee* by Dee Brown, © 1970 by Dee Brown. Reprinted by permission of Sterling Lord
Literistic, Inc. CHIEF SEATTLE: Extracts from *A Cherokee Feast of Days*, by Joyce
Sequichie Hifler, Council Oak Books, 1992. JOYCE SEQUICHE HIFLER: Extracts from *A
Cherokee Feast of Days*, ed. by Joyce Sequiche Hifler, Council Oak Books, 1992. REX LEE
JIM: Extract from *Dancing Voices*, ed. Rex Lee Jim, Peter Pauper Press, 1994. © 1994 Rex
Lee Jim. Used with permission of the author. Extracts from *The Haudenosaunee Address to
the Western World, 1977* and *The Haudenosaunee Declaration 1979.* LUTHER STANDING
BEAR: Extracts from *Land of the Spotted Eagle*, published by The University of Nebraska
Press. Used with permission. CHARLES EASTMAN: Extracts from *The Soul of the Indian*,
Houghton Mifflin, Boston, 1911. STARHAWK: "Earth Mother, Star Mother," by Starhawk
from The Spiral Dance published by Harpers & Row. Used with permission of Ken
Sherman Associates and HarperCollins Publishers, Inc.

In
beauty
may
I
walk...

A HELEN EXLEY
GIFTBOOK

NEW YORK • WATFORD, UK

IN BEAUTY MAY I WALK

In beauty
may I walk
All day long
may I walk
Through the returning seasons
may I walk
Beautifully will I possess again
Beautifully birds
Beautifully joyful birds
On the trail marked with pollen
may I walk
With grasshoppers about my feet
may I walk
With dew about my feet
may I walk
With beauty may I walk

With beauty before me

may I walk

With beauty behind me

may I walk

With beauty above me

may I walk

With beauty all around me

may I walk

In old age, wandering on a trail of

beauty, lively,

may I walk

In old age, wandering on a trail of

beauty, living again,

may I walk,

It is finished in beauty.

It is finished in beauty.

FROM THE NAVAJO

The

trail

is

beautiful.

Be

still.

ANONYMOUS,
Dakota

Training began with children who were taught to sit still and enjoy it. They were taught to use their organs of smell, to look where there was apparently nothing to see, and to listen intently when all seemingly was quiet. A child who cannot sit still is a half-developed child.

LUTHER STANDING BEAR (1868-1939),
Oglala Sioux chief

Silence is the absolute poise or balance of body, mind and spirit. The man who preserves his selfhood is ever calm and unshaken by the storms of existence.... If you ask him: "What is silence?" he will answer: "It is the Great Mystery. The holy silence is His voice." If you ask: "What are the fruits of silence?" he will say: "They are self-control, true courage or endurance, patience, dignity and reverence. Silence is the cornerstone of character."

OHIYESA (Dr. Charles Eastman),
Santee Sioux

Once you have heard the meadowlark and caught the scent of fresh-plowed earth, peace cannot escape you.

SEQUICHIE

...All sounds, all fears, all loves.

We are all creators. We breathe. To speak is to form breath and to make manifest sound into the world. As I write I create myself again and again. Re-Create. And breathe. And I see that I am not one voice, but many: all colors, all sounds, all fears, all loves.

JOY HARJO,
Creek

IN REVERENCE OF NATURE

Whenever, in the course of the daily hunt the red hunter comes upon a scene that is strikingly beautiful or sublime – a black thundercloud with the rainbow's glowing arch above the mountain; a white waterfall in the heart of a green gorge; a vast prairie tinged with the blood-red of a sunset – he pauses for an instant in the attitude of worship.

OHIYESA (Dr. Charles Eastman),
Santee Sioux

Remember, remember the sacredness
of things running streams and
dwellings
the young within the nest
a hearth for sacred fire
the holy flame.

OMAHA INDIAN CHANT

He wakes at daybreak, puts on his moccasins and steps down to the water's edge. Here he throws handfuls of clear, cold water into his face, or plunges in bodily. After the bath, he stands erect before the advancing dawn, facing the sun as it dances upon the horizon, and offers his unspoken orison. His mate may precede or follow him in his devotions, but never accompanies him. Each soul must meet the morning sun, the new sweet earth and the Great Silence alone!

OHIYESA (Dr. Charles Eastman),
Santee Sioux

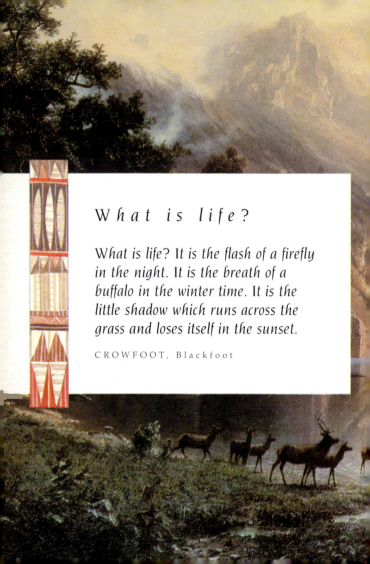

What is life?

What is life? It is the flash of a firefly in the night. It is the breath of a buffalo in the winter time. It is the little shadow which runs across the grass and loses itself in the sunset.

CROWFOOT, Blackfoot

The land
I stand on
is my body....

SAM JONES,
Miccosukee Seminole

Hear me, four quarters of the world – a
relative I am! Give me the strength to walk
the soft earth, a relative to all that is!
Give me the eyes to see and the strength
to understand, that I may be like you. With
your power only can I face the winds.

BLACK ELK (1863-1950),
Oglala Sioux

The American Indian is of the soil, whether it be the region of forests, plains, pueblos, or mesas. He fits into the landscape, for the hand that fashioned the continent also fashioned the man. He once grew as naturally as the wild sunflowers; he belongs just as the buffalo belonged....

LUTHER STANDING BEAR (1868-1939), Oglala Sioux chief

The earth and myself are of one mind. The measure of the land and the measure of our bodies are the same....

CHIEF JOSEPH (1830-1904), Nez Percé

Take the breath of the new dawn and make it part of you. It will give you strength.

HOPI

THE TOUCH
OF THE EARTH

The old people came literally to love the soil and they sat or reclined on the ground with a feeling of being close to a mothering power. It was good for the skin to touch the earth and the old people liked to remove their moccasins and walk with bare feet on the sacred earth. Their tipis were built upon the earth and their altars were made of earth. The birds that flew in the air came to rest upon the earth and it was the final abiding place of all things that lived and grew. The soil was soothing, strengthening, cleansing and healing. That is why the old Indian still sits upon the earth instead of propping himself up away from its life-giving forces. For him, to sit or lie upon the ground is to be able to think more deeply and feel more keenly.

LUTHER STANDING BEAR (1868-1939),
Oglala Sioux chief

Our bare feet are conscious
of the sympathetic touch
of our ancestors
as we walk over this earth.

CHIEF SEATTLE
Suquamish / Duwamish

... healthy feet can hear
the very heart of Holy Earth....

SITTING BULL
(Tatanka Yotanka),
Sioux warrior

Be careful when speaking.
You create the world around you
with your words.

FROM THE NAVAJO

Conversation was never begun at once, nor in a hurried manner. No one was quick with a question, no matter how important, and no one was pressed for an answer. A pause giving time for thought was the truly courteous way of beginning and conducting a conversation. Silence was meaningful with the Lakota, and his granting a space of silence to the speech-maker and his own moment of silence before talking was done in the practice of true politeness and regard for the rule that, "thought comes before speech."

LUTHER STANDING BEAR (1868-1939),
Oglala Sioux chief

There is a dignity about the social intercourse
of old Indians which reminds me of a stroll
through a winter forest.

COCHISE
Chiricahua Apache

No talk is ever given without first indicating
your humility. "I am an ignorant man; I am a
poor man" – all the talks start this way – "I
don't know nearly as much as you men sitting
around here, but I would like to offer my
humble opinion," and then he'll knock you
down with logic and wisdom.

ALLEN C. QUETONE,
Kiowa

Listen! Or your tongue will make you deaf.

CHEROKEE SAYING

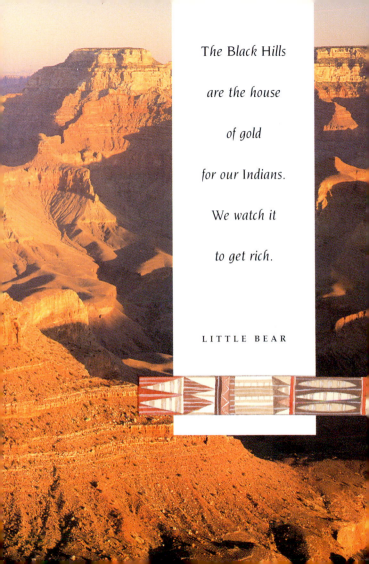

The Black Hills

are the house

of gold

for our Indians.

We watch it

to get rich.

LITTLE BEAR

WE ARE ALL EQUAL

THE COLOR OF SKIN MAKES NO DIFFERENCE. WHAT IS GOOD AND JUST FOR ONE IS GOOD AND JUST FOR THE OTHER, AND THE GREAT SPIRIT MADE ALL MEN BROTHERS.

WHITE SHIELD

... YOU SHOULD UNDERSTAND THE WAY IT WAS BACK THEN, BECAUSE IT IS THE SAME EVEN NOW.

LESLIE MARMON SILKO,
Laguna

That hand is not the color of your hand, but if I pierce it I shall feel pain. The blood that will follow from mine will be the same color as yours. The Great Spirit made us both.

LUTHER STANDING BEAR (1868-1939)
Oglala Sioux chief

Great Spirit, Great Spirit, my Grandfather, all over the earth the faces of living things are all alike.... Look upon these faces of children without number and with children in their arms, that they may face the winds and walk the good road to the day of quiet.

BLACK ELK (1863-1950),
Oglala Sioux

We are all flowers in the Great Spirit's garden. We share a common root, and the root is Mother Earth. The garden is beautiful because it has different colors in it, and those colors represent different traditions and cultural backgrounds.

GRANDFATHER DAVID MONONGYE,
Hopi

L O V E

Love is something you
and I must have. We
must have it because our
spirit feeds upon it. We
must have it because
without it we become
weak and faint. Without
love our self-esteem
weakens. Without it our
courage fails. Without
love we can no longer
look confidently at the
world. We turn inward
and begin to feed upon
our own personalities,
and little by little we
destroy it ourselves.
With it we are creative.
With it we march
tirelessly. With it, and
with it alone, we are able
to sacrifice for others.

CHIEF DAN GEORGE

Why do you take

by force what you

could obtain

by love?

POWHATAN

TEACH US LOVE, COMPASSION, HONOR

Grandfather,
Look at our brokenness.
We know that in all creation
Only the human family
Has strayed from the sacred way.
We know that we are the ones
Who are divided
And we are the ones
Who must come back together
To walk in the sacred way
Grandfather,
Sacred One,
Teach us love, compassion, honor
That we may heal the earth
And heal each other.

OJIBWAY PRAYER

The Italian explorer Christopher
Columbus simply verified what
Indians already knew when he
desribed them as *un gente que
vive en dios* – a people who live
in God. As children *en dios* – in

God, they must come to
understand that they may yet
save the world. It must begin
with simple, sanctifying words
from the tips of their tongues.

Helping save the world from
cultural genocide for me must
begin with the sacred words, *en
dios – indios* – in God. I am an
American Indian, not a Native
American.

REX LEE JIM

IN TIMES OF DANGER

The idea of full dress in preparation for a battle comes not from a belief that it will add to the fighting ability. The preparation is for death, in case that should be the result of the conflict. Every Indian wants to look his best when he goes to meet the Great Spirit, so the dressing up is done whether an imminent danger is an oncoming battle or a sickness or injury at times of peace.

WOODEN LEG,
Cheyenne

PEACE
BETWEEN ALL PEOPLES

Brothers and sisters: We bring to your thought and minds that right-minded human beings seek to promote above all else the life of all things. We direct to your minds that peace is not merely the absence of war, but the constant effort to maintain harmonious existence between all peoples, from individual to individual, and between humans and the other beings of this planet. We point out to you that a spiritual consciousness is the path to survival of humankind.

THE HAUDENOSAUNEE
DECLARATION, 1979

Now we are in a critical stage of our spiritual, moral and technological development as nations. All life is precariously balanced. We must remember that all things on Mother Earth have spirit and are intricately related. The Lakota prophecy of Mending the Sacred Hoop of all nations has begun. May we find, in the ancient wisdom of the indigenous nations, the spirit and courage to mend and heal.

ARVOL LOOKING HORSE,
Lakota

I WILL BE STILL
AND STEADY...

If, like a Cherokee warrior, I can look at the new year as an opportunity to stand on new ground, then strength and courage are on my side. I will remember that things do work out, bodies do heal, relationships mend – not because I said it, but because I believe it.

But it is time to make things right, to stay on the path. As water runs fresh and free from the woodland spring, so new life and meaning will bubble up from my own inner source. I will be still and steady, because there is nothing to be gained by showing fear in a chaotic world.

JOYCE SEQUICHIE HIFLER

THE CITY

Hills are always more beautiful than stone buildings, you know. Living in a city is an artificial existence. Lots of people hardly ever feel real soil under their feet, see plants grow except in flower pots, or get far enough beyond the street light to catch the enchantment of a night sky studded with stars. When people live far from scenes of the Great Spirit's making, it's easy for them to forget his laws.

WALKING BUFFALO (Tatanga Mani),
(1871-1967)

I was born upon the prairie, where the wind blew free, and there was nothing to break the light of the sun. I was born where there were no enclosures, and where everything drew a free breath....

TEN BEARS,
Yamparethka Comanche chief

There is no quiet place in [your] cities, no place to hear the leaves of spring or the rustle of insects' wings.... The Indians prefer the soft sound of the wind darting over the face of the pond, the smell of the wind itself cleansed by a midday rain, or scented with pinon pine. The air is precious to the red man, for all things share the same breath — the animals, the trees, the man. Like a man who has been dying for many days, a man in your city is numb to the stench.

CHIEF SEATTLE,
Suquamish/Duwamish

You might as well expect rivers to run backward as that any man who was born a free man should be contented when penned up and denied liberty.

CHIEF JOSEPH (1830-1904)
Nez Percé

It was our belief that the love of possessions is a weakness to be overcome. Its appeal is to the material part, and if allowed its way, it will in time disturb one's spiritual balance. Therefore, children must early learn the beauty of generosity. They are taught to give what they prize most, that they may taste the happiness of giving.

OHIYESA (Dr. Charles Eastman), Santee Sioux

... one of the things we have learned in our sobriety is the only way we can keep what we have, or feeling good about ourselves, is to give it away.

HAROLD BELMONT, Suquamish/Songee

CARE FOR THE LAND

Being born as humans to this earth is a very sacred trust. We have a sacred responsibility because of the special gift we have, which is beyond the fine gifts of the plant life, the fish, the woodlands, the birds, and all the other living things on earth. We are able to take care of them.

AUDREY SHENANDOAH,
Onondaga

The people who are living on this planet need to break with the narrow concept of human liberation, and begin to see liberation as something that needs to be extended to the whole of the natural world. What is needed is the liberation of all things that support life – the air, the waters, the trees – all the things which support the sacred web of life.

FROM THE HAUDENOSAUNEE ADDRESS TO
THE WESTERN WORLD, 1977

EVERY PART OF THIS SOIL IS SACRED...
EVERY HILLSIDE, EVERY VALLEY, EVERY
PLAIN AND GROVE... RESPONDS LOVINGLY
TO (OUR) FOOTSTEPS....

CHIEF SEATTLE
Suquamish/Duwamish

Any pretty pebble was valuable to me then,
every growing tree an object of reverence.

OHIYESA (Dr. Charles Eastman),
Santee Sioux

All life is Wakan. So also is everything which
exhibits power, whether in action, as the winds
and drifting clouds, or in passive endurance, as
the boulder by the wayside. For even the
commonest sticks and stones have a spiritual
essence which must be reverenced as a
manifestation of the all-pervading mysterious
power that fills the universe.

FRANCIS LAFLESCHE
Osage

Everywhere is the center of the world.
Everything is sacred.

BLACK ELK (1863-1950),
Oglala Sioux

THE INDIAN LOVED TO WORSHIP.
FROM BIRTH TO DEATH HE REVERED HIS
SURROUNDINGS. HE CONSIDERED
HIMSELF BORN IN THE LUXURIOUS LAP
OF MOTHER EARTH AND NO PLACE TO
HIM WAS HUMBLE. THERE WAS NOTHING
BETWEEN HIM AND THE BIG HOLY.
THE CONTACT WAS IMMEDIATE AND
PERSONAL AND THE BLESSINGS OF
WAKAN TANKA FLOWED OVER THE
INDIAN LIKE RAIN SHOWERED
FROM THE SKY.

LUTHER STANDING BEAR
(1868-1939),
Oglala Sioux chief

THIS LAND
WILL ALWAYS BE HERE

Our land is more valuable than your money. It will last forever. It will not even perish by the flames of fire. As long as the sun shines and the waters flow, this land will be here to give life to men and animals. We cannot sell the lives of men and animals; therefore we cannot sell this land. It was put here for us by the Great Spirit and we cannot sell it because it does not belong to us. You can count your money and burn it within the nod of a buffalo's head, but only the Great Spirit can count the grains of sand and the blades of grass of these plains. As a present to you, we will give you anything we have that you can take with you; but the land, never.

A CHIEF
OF ONE OF
THE BLACKFEET
BANDS

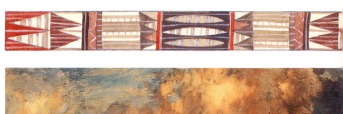

Oh, yes, I went to the white man's schools. I learned to read from school books, newspapers, and the Bible. But in time I found that these were not enough. Civilized people depend too much on man-made printed pages. I turn to the Great Spirit's book which is the whole of creation. You can read a big part of that book if you study nature. You know, if you take all your books, lay them out under the sun, and let the snow and rain and insects work on them for a while, there will be nothing left. But the Great Spirit has provided you and me with an opportunity to study in nature's university the forests, the rivers, the mountains and the animals which include us.

WALKING BUFFALO (1871-1967) (Tatanga Mani), Stoney Indian

He knew that man's heart, away from nature, becomes hard.

LUTHER STANDING BEAR (1868-1939),
Oglala Sioux chief

I am going to venture that the man who sat on the ground in his tipi meditating on life and its meaning, accepting the kinship of all creatures, and acknowledging unity with the universe of things was infusing into his being the true essence of civilization. And when native man left off this form of development, his humanization was retarded in growth.

LUTHER STANDING BEAR (1868-1939),
Oglala Sioux chief

As a child I understood how to give; I have forgotten this grace since I became civilized.

OHIYESA (Dr. Charles Eastman),
Santee Sioux

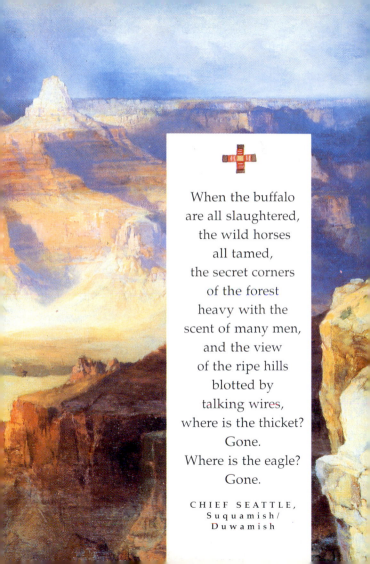

When the buffalo
are all slaughtered,
the wild horses
all tamed,
the secret corners
of the forest
heavy with the
scent of many men,
and the view
of the ripe hills
blotted by
talking wires,
where is the thicket?
Gone.
Where is the eagle?
Gone.

CHIEF SEATTLE,
Suquamish/
Duwamish

Everything's a circle. We're each responsible for our own actions. It will come back.

BETTY LAVERDURE
Ojibway

To honor and respect means to think of the land and the water and plants and animals who live here as having a right equal to our own to be here. We are not the supreme and all-knowing beings, living at the top of the pinnacle of evolution, but in fact we are members of the sacred hoop of life, along with the trees and rocks, the coyotes and the eagles and fish and toads, that each fulfills its purpose. They each perform their given task in the sacred hoop, and we have one, too.

WOLF SONG,
Abenaki

"THE SPIRAL DANCE"

Earth mother, star mother,
You who are called by a thousand names,
May all remember we are cells in your body
    and dance together.
You are the grain and the loaf
That sustains us each day.
And as you are patient with our struggles to
    learn
So shall we be patient with ourselves and
    each other.
We are radiant light and sacred dark – the
    balance –
You are the embrace that heartens
And the freedom beyond fear.
Within you we are born, we grow,
    live, and die –
You bring us around the circle to rebirth,
Within us you dance
Forever.

STARHAWK

... THE SEVENTH GENERATION TO COME

In our way of life, in our government, with every decision we make, we always keep in mind the Seventh Generation to come. It's our job to see that the people coming ahead, the generations still unborn, have a world no worse than ours – and hopefully better. When we walk upon Mother Earth we always plant our feet carefully because we know the faces of our future generations are looking up at us from beneath the ground. We never forget them.

OREN LYONS,
Onondaga Faithkeeper

Tell them
how we loved
all that was beautiful.

NATIVE AMERICAN

I was born in nature's wild domain....
I am one of nature's children. I have always
admired her. She shall be my glory....
And wherever I see her, emotions of
pleasure roll in my breast, and swell and
burst like waves on the shore of the ocean,
in prayer and praise to Him who has placed
me in her hand.

GEORGE COPWAY

" . . . WITH A BROKEN WING"

I see as in a vision
the dying spark
of our council fires,
the ashes cold and white.
I see no longer
the curling smoke
rising from our lodge poles.
I hear no longer
the songs of women
as they prepare the meal.
The antelope have gone.
The buffalo wallos are empty.
Only the wail of the coyote is heard....
We are like birds
with a broken wing.

CHIEF PLENTY-COUPS

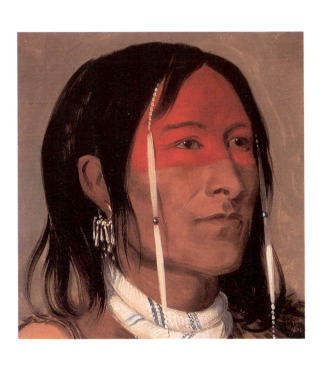

WITH CLEAN HANDS

O Great Spirit,
Whose voice I hear in the winds,
And whose breath gives life to all the world,
hear me!
Let me walk in beauty, and make my eyes
ever behold the red and purple sunset. Make
my hands respect the things you have made
and my ears sharp to hear your voice.
Let me learn the lessons you have hidden in
every leaf and rock.
I seek strength, not to be greater than
my brother, but to fight my greatest
enemy – myself.
Make me always ready to come to you with
clean hands and straight eyes.
So when life fades, as the fading sunset, my
spirit may come to you without shame.

NATIVE AMERICAN

LIFE'S DRUM

From the beginning there were drums,
beating out world rhythm —
the booming, never-failing
tide on the beach;
the four seasons,
gliding smoothly, one from the other;
when the birds come,
when they go,
the bear hibernating
for his winter sleep.
Unfathomable the why,
yet all in perfect time.
Watch the heartbeat in your wrist
— a precise pulsing beat
of life's drum.

JIMALEE BURTON,
Cherokee